Studies in the Scriptures

PRISON EPISTLES

WORKBOOK AND MECHANICAL OUTLINE

Ephesians, Philippians, Colossians, Philemon

John T. Stevenson

Redeemer Publishing

© John Stevenson, 2015

Reprinted 2017

Redeemer Publishing
Hollywood, FL
www.RedeemerPublishing.com

Translation adapted from the American Standard Version
1903

TABLE OF CONTENTS

Books by John Stevenson:

Ancient History: *A Framework for the Bible*
Doctrines of the Bible: *Outlines in Systematic Theology*
Facing the Flames: *A Fire Fighter's Meditations on the Spiritual Life*
First Corinthians: *Striving for Unity*
Ecclesiastes: *A Spiritual Journey*
Ephesians: *The Wealth & Walk of the Christian*
Galatians: *Our Freedom in Christ*
Genesis: *The Book of Beginnings, Volume 1*
Hebrews: *The Supremacy of the Savior*
Historical Books of the Old Testament: *One God, One People, One Land*
James: *A Faith that Works*
Joshua, Judges, and Ruth: *Victory, Defeat, and Hope in an Age of Heroes*
Luke: *In the Footsteps of the Savior*
Mark: *The Servant Who Came to Save*
Preaching from the Minor Prophets to a Postmodern Congregation
Romans: *The Radical Righteousness of God*
A Survey of the Old Testament: *The Bible Jesus Used*

EPHESIANS - THE BODY OF CHRIST

1:1	1:15	2:1	3:1	4:1	4:17	5:17	6:10
Wealth of the Christian				Walk of the Christian			
Praise	Paul's prayer	Past versus present	Paul's prayer	Call for unity	Call for new walk		Call for new armor
Blessings in Christ		Experience of salvation	Growth	Christian Conduct			Armor
We in Christ				Christ in us			
Work of God				Walk of the Christian			
Heavenly Standing				Earthly Walk			
Know		Remember	Grow	Walk			Stand

The first three chapters describe the wealth of the Christian. Paul speaks seven times of the "riches" and the "inheritance" that we have in Christ.

1:7	"according to the riches of His grace"
1:11	"we have obtained an inheritance"
1:14	"a pledge of our inheritance"
1:18	"the riches of the glory of His inheritance"
2:7	"the surpassing riches of His grace"
3:8	"the unfathomable riches of His grace"
3:16	"the riches of His glory"

Chapters 4-6 give the walk of the Christian. We are exhorted five times to walk in a proper way (in chapter 6 this is changed to "stand firm").

4:1	"walk in a manner worthy of the calling with which you have been called"
4:17	"walk no longer just as the Gentiles also walk"
5:2	"walk in love"
5:8	"walk as children of light"
5:15	"be careful how you walk"
6:11	"stand firm against the schemes of the devil"
6:13	"stand firm"
6:14	"Stand firm"

Ephesians is a letter about the church - the body of Christ. The church is described here as...

- A body (Ephesians 1:22-23;4:4; 4:16).
- A building (Ephesians 2:19-22).
- A bride (Ephesians 5:25-27; 5:32).

Characteristics of the Epistle

- There are very few personal notes or biographical references within the book.

- There are a number of very long sentences within the epistle.
  Ephesians 1:3-14
    — Ephesians 1:15-23
    — Ephesians 3:1-7
    — Ephesians 3:8-12
    — Ephesians 4:11-16

1:1   Paul,
        an apostle
                of Christ Jesus
                through the will of God,
        to the saints
                who are
                        at Ephesus,
                        and
                        faithful in Christ Jesus:

1:2   Grace to you
        and
        peace
                from
                        God our Father
                        and
                        the Lord Jesus Christ.

1:3   Blessed be the God and Father of our Lord Jesus Christ,
>who
>has blessed us
>>with every spiritual blessing
>>in the heavenlies
>>in Christ:

1:4   even as
>he chose us
>>in him
>>before the foundation of the world,
>>>that
>>>we should be holy and unblemished before him in love:

1:5   having predestined us
>>>into adoption as sons
>>>through Jesus Christ
>>>into himself,
>>according to the good pleasure of his will,

1:6   to the praise of the glory of his grace,
>>which he freely bestowed on us in the Beloved:

1:7   in whom
>>>we have
>>>>our redemption through his blood,
>>>>the forgiveness of our trespasses,
>>>>>according to
>>>>>the riches of his grace,

1:8   which
>>>>>he made to abound toward us
>>>>>>in all wisdom and prudence,

1:9   having made known unto us the mystery of his will,
>>>>>according to
>>>>>his good pleasure
>>>>>>which
>>>>>>he purposed in him

1:10   into an administration
>>>>>>>of the fulness of the times,
>>>>>>to sum up all things in Christ,
>>>>>>>the things in the heavens,
>>>>>>>and
>>>>>>>the things upon the earth;
>>>>>>in him, I say,

1:11 in whom also
   we were made a heritage,
   having been predestined
    according to
    the purpose of him
     who
     works all things after the counsel of his will;
1:12 to the end that we should be unto the praise of his glory,
    we who had before hoped in Christ:
1:13   in whom you also,
     having heard the word of the truth,
      the gospel of your salvation,
    – in whom,
    having also believed,
    you were sealed with the Holy Spirit of promise,
1:14   which
      is an earnest of our inheritance,
    into
    the redemption of God's own possession,
    to the praise of his glory.

1:15   For this cause
        I also,
            having heard of
                the faith in the Lord Jesus
                    which
                    is among you,
            and
            the love
                which
                you show toward all the saints,
1:16   do not cease to give thanks for you,
        making mention of you in my prayers;
1:17   that
    the God of our Lord Jesus Christ,
    the Father of glory,
    may give to you
        a spirit of
            wisdom
            and
            revelation
        in the knowledge of him;

1:18   having enlightened the eyes of your heart,
       that you may know
           what is the hope of his calling,
           what are the riches of the glory of his inheritance in the saints,
1:19   and
           what the exceeding greatness of his power toward us who believe,
              according to
           that working of the strength of his might
1:20   which he worked in Christ,
         when he
           raised him from the dead,
           and
           made him to sit at his right hand in the heavenly places,
1:21   far above all
                 rule,
                 and
                 authority,
                 and
                 power,
                 and
                 dominion,
                 and
                 every name that is named,
                    not only in this age,
                    but
                    also in that which is to come:
1:22   and
            he put all things in subjection under his feet,
           and
            gave him to be head over all things to the church,
1:23   which
              is his body,
              the fulness of him that fills all in all.

2:1   And you,
        being dead in your trespasses and sins,
2:2   in which
          you previously walked
            according to the age of this age,
            according to the prince
              of the power of the air,
              of the spirit now working in the sons of disobedience;
2:3   among whom
              we also all once lived in the lust of our flesh,
              doing the desires
                of the flesh
                and
                of the mind,
              and
              were by nature children of wrath,
              even as the rest: --
2:4   but God,
        being rich in mercy,
        because of His great love with which He loved us,
2:5   even when we were dead
          through
          our trespasses,
     made us alive
        together with Christ
            (by grace have you been saved),
2:6   and
    raised us up with Him,
    and
    made us to sit with Him
        in the heavenly places,
        in Christ Jesus:
2:7   that
      in the ages to come
      he might show the exceeding riches of his grace
         in kindness toward us
         in Christ Jesus:

2:8	For
	by grace you have been saved
	through faith;
	and
	that not of yourselves,
	it is the gift of God;
2:9	not of works,
	that
	no one should boast.
2:10	For
	we are His doing,
	created in Christ Jesus for good works,
	which
	God prepared beforehand
	that
	we should walk in them.

2:11   Therefore remember,
      that once you,
            the Gentiles in the flesh,
                who
                are called Uncircumcision
                by that which is called Circumcision,
                    in the flesh,
                    made by hands;
2:12   that you were at that time
            separate from Christ,
            alienated from the commonwealth of Israel,
            and
            strangers from the covenants of the promise,
            having no hope
            and
            without God in the world.
2:13   But now
      in Christ Jesus
   you
      who
      once were far off
   are made near
      in
      the blood of Christ.

2:14   For
      he is our peace,
         who
         made both one,
         and destroyed the middle wall of partition,

2:15   having abolished in the flesh
         the enmity,
         even the law of commandments contained in ordinances;
      that
      of the two he might create in himself one new man,
      making peace;

2:16   and
      might reconcile them both in one body to God through the cross,
      having put to death the enmity:

2:17   and
      he came and preached
         peace to you that were far off,
         and
         peace to them that were near:

2:18   for
      through him we both have our access in one Spirit into the Father.

2:19   So then
      you are no longer strangers and sojourners,
      but you are
         fellow-citizens with the saints,
         and
         of the household of God,

2:20   being built upon the foundation of
               the apostles
               and
               prophets,
         Christ Jesus himself being the chief corner stone;

2:21   in whom each several building,
               fitly framed together,
            is growing into a holy temple in the Lord;

2:22   in whom
               you also are being built together for a habitation of God
                  in the Spirit.

3:1 For this cause
I Paul,
    the prisoner of Christ Jesus on behalf of you Gentiles, --
3:2   if so be that you have heard of the administration of that grace of God
    which was given me toward you;
3:3 how that by revelation was made known to me the mystery,
    as I wrote before in few words,
3:4 whereby,
    when you read,
    you can perceive my understanding in the mystery of Christ;
3:5   which
      in other generations was not made known unto the sons of men,
      as it has now been revealed
        to
          his holy apostles
          and
          prophets
        in the Spirit;
3:6   that
    the Gentiles are
        fellow-heirs,
        and
        fellow-members of the body,
        and
        fellow-partakers of the promise in Christ Jesus through the gospel,
3:7   of which
          I was made a minister,
            according to
            the gift of that grace of God which was given me
              according to
              the working of his power.

3:8 Unto me,
   who
   am less than the least of all saints,
  was this grace given,
  to preach to the Gentiles the unsearchable riches of Christ;
3:9 and
  to make all men see what is the administration of the mystery
   which
   for ages has been hidden in God
     who
     created all things;
3:10 to the intent that now
   unto the principalities and the powers in the heavenly places
   might be made known through the church
   the manifold wisdom of God,
3:11   according to
   the eternal purpose
    which
    he purposed in Christ Jesus our Lord:
3:12   in whom
     we have
       boldness
       and
       access in confidence
    through
    our faith in him.

3:13   Therefore I ask that you may not faint at my tribulations for you,
        which
        are your glory.

3:14   For this cause
  I bow my knees unto the Father,

3:15   from whom
        every family in heaven and on earth is named,

3:16   that
  he would grant you,
        according to the riches of his glory,
  that
  you might be strengthened
    with power
    through his Spirit
    in the inner man;

3:17   that
  Christ may dwell in your hearts through faith;
  to the end that you,
        being rooted and grounded in love,

3:18   may be strong to apprehend with all the saints
    what is the
            breadth
            and
            length
            and
            height
            and
            depth,

3:19   and
    to know the love of Christ which passes knowledge,
           that
           you may be filled with all the fulness of God.

3:20   Now
  unto Him that is able to do exceeding abundantly above all that we ask or think,
        according to the power that works in us,

3:21   unto him be the glory
    in the church
    and
    in Christ Jesus
  unto all generations for ever and ever.   Amen.

4:1 I therefore,
    the prisoner in the Lord,
  exhort you to walk worthy of the calling with which you were called,

4:2   with all lowliness and meekness,
    with longsuffering,
    forbearing one another in love;

4:3   giving diligence to keep the unity of the Spirit in the bond of peace.

4:4 There is
  one body,
  and
  one Spirit,
  even as also you were called in one hope of your calling;

4:5 one Lord,
  one faith,
  one baptism,

4:6 one God and Father of all,
    who is
      over all,
      and
      through all,
      and
      in all.

4:7   But
        to each one of us the grace was given
            according to
            the measure of the gift of Christ.

4:8   Therefore he says,
            When He ascended on high,
            He led captivity captive,
            And gave gifts to men.

4:9   (Now this,
               He ascended,
               what is it but that he also descended into the lower parts of the earth?

4:10   He that descended is the same also that ascended
                 far above all the heavens,
                   that
                   he might fill all things.)

4:11   And
       he gave
              some to be apostles;
              and
              some, prophets;
              and
              some, evangelists;
              and
              some, pastors and teachers;

4:12   for the perfecting of the saints,
     to the work of ministering,
     to the building up of the body of Christ:

4:13   until we all attain to the unity
              of the faith,
              and
              of the knowledge of the Son of God,
       to a mature man,
       to the measure of the stature of the fulness of Christ:

4:14   that
       we may be no longer children,
           tossed to and fro
           and
           carried about
              with every wind of teaching,
              by the sleight of men, in craftiness,
              after the wiles of error;

4:15   but
       truthing in love,
           we may grow up in all things into him,
              who
              is the head,
              even Christ;

4:16   from whom
              all the body fitly framed and knit together
              through that which every joint supplies,
              according to
              the working in due measure of each individual part,
              makes the growth of the body unto the building up of itself
              in love.

4:17 This I say therefore,
and
testify in the Lord,
    that
    you no longer walk as the Gentiles also walk,
        in the vanity of their mind,
4:18   being darkened in their understanding,
        alienated from the life of God,
            because of the ignorance that is in them,
            because of the hardening of their heart;
4:19 who
being past feeling
gave themselves up to lasciviousness,
to work all uncleanness with greediness.
4:20 But
you did not so learn Christ;
4:21   if it be that you
        heard him,
        and
        were taught in him,
    even as truth is in Jesus:
4:22 that
you put away regarding your former manner of life, the old man,
        that
        turns corrupt after the lusts of deceit;
4:23 and that
you be renewed in the spirit of your mind,
4:24 and
put on the new man,
    that
    after God has been created in righteousness and holiness of truth.

4:25   Therefore,
>   putting away falsehood,
>   speak truth each one with his neighbor:
>>   for
>>   we are members one of another.

4:26   Be angry,
and
sin not:
>   let not the sun go down upon your wrath:

4:27   neither give place to the devil.

4:28   Let him that stole steal no more:
but
rather let him labor,
>   working with his hands the thing that is good,
>>   that
>>   he may have whereof to give to him that has need.

4:29   Let no corrupt speech proceed out of your mouth,
but
such as is good for edifying as the need may be,
>   that
>   it may give grace to them that hear.

4:30   And
do not grieve the Holy Spirit of God,
>   in whom you were sealed unto the day of redemption.

4:31   Let all
>   bitterness,
>   and wrath,
>   and anger,
>   and clamor,
>   and railing,
be put away from you,
>   with all malice:

4:32   and
be kind to one another,
>   tenderhearted,
>   forgiving each other,
>   even as God also in Christ forgave you.

5:1   Therefore be imitators of God, as beloved children;

5:2   and

walk in love,

    even as Christ also

        loved you,

        and

        gave Himself up for us,

            an offering

            and

            a sacrifice to God for a sweet-smelling aroma.

5:3   But

    fornication,

    and

    all uncleanness,

    or covetousness,

let it not even be named among you,

    as is proper for saints;

5:4   nor filthiness,

    nor foolish talking,

    or jesting,

        which are not appropriate:

but

rather giving of thanks.

5:5   For seeing this, you know that

        no fornicator,

        nor unclean person,

        nor covetous man, who is an idolater,

    has any inheritance in the kingdom of Christ and God.

5:6   Let no man deceive you with empty words:

    for because of these things

    the wrath of God comes upon the sons of disobedience.

5:7   Therefore
        do not be partakers with them;
5:8   for
        you were formerly darkness,
        but
        are now light in the Lord:
        walk as children of light
5:9   (for the fruit of the light is in all goodness and righteousness and truth),
5:10   demonstrating what is well-pleasing unto the Lord;
5:11   and
        have no fellowship with the unfruitful works of darkness,
        but
        rather even reprove them;
5:12   for
        it is a shame even to speak of the things which are done by them in secret.
5:13   But
        all things when they are reproved are made manifest by the light:
         for
        everything that is made manifest is light.
5:14   Therefore he says,
            Awake, you who sleeps,
            and arise from the dead,
            and Christ shall shine upon you.

5:15 Look therefore carefully how you walk,
> not as unwise,
> but
> as wise;

5:16 redeeming the time,
>> because
>> the days are evil.

5:17 Therefore
be not foolish,
but
understand what the will of the Lord is.

5:18 And
be not drunken with wine,
> wherein is wastefulness,
but
be filled with the Spirit;

5:19 > speaking one to another
>>> in psalms
>>> and
>>> hymns
>>> and
>>> spiritual songs,
> singing
> and
> making melody with your heart to the Lord;

5:20 > giving thanks always for all things in the name of our Lord Jesus Christ
>>> to God,
>>> even the Father;

5:21 > subjecting yourselves one to another in the fear of Christ;

5:22 >> wives to your own husbands, as unto the Lord,

5:23 >>> because
>>> the husband is the head of the wife,
>>>> as Christ also is the head of the church,
>>>>> being himself the savior of the body.

5:24 >>> but
>>> as the church is subject to Christ,
>>> so let the wives also be to their husbands in everything.

5:25 Husbands,
love your wives,
even as Christ also
> loved the church,
> and
> gave himself up for it;
5:26
>> so that
>> he might sanctify it,
>> having cleansed it by the washing of water with the word,
5:27
>>> that
>>> he might present the church to himself a glorious church,
>>>> not having spot or wrinkle or any such thing;
>>>> but
>>>> that it should be holy and without blemish.

5:28 Even so
husbands ought also to love their own wives
> as their own bodies.
He that loves his own wife loves himself:
5:29
> for
no man ever hated his own flesh;
but
nourishes and cherishes it,
> even as Christ also the church;
5:30
>> because
>> we are members of his body.
5:31
>>> For this cause
>>> a man shall leave his father and mother,
>>> and
>>> shall cleave to his wife;
>>> and
>>> the two shall become one flesh.
5:32
>> This mystery is great:
>> but
>> I speak in regard of Christ and of the church.
5:33 However
let each one of you
> love his own wife even as himself;
> and
> that the wife fear her husband.

6:1   Children,
      obey your parents in the Lord: for this is right.
6:2   Honor your father and mother
          (which is the first commandment with promise),
6:3   that
          it may be well with you,
          and
          you may live long on the earth.
6:4   And,
   you fathers,
      provoke not your children to wrath:
      but
      nurture them in the chastening and admonition of the Lord.
6:5   Slaves,
      be obedient unto them that according to the flesh are your masters,
          with fear and trembling,
          in singleness of your heart,
             as unto Christ;
6:6   not in the way of eye-service,
             as men-pleasers;
      but
      as slaves of Christ,
        doing the will of God from the heart;
6:7   with good will doing service,
             as unto the Lord,
             and
             not unto men:
6:8   knowing that whatsoever good thing each one does,
        the same shall he receive again from the Lord,
          whether he be bond or free.
6:9   And,
   you masters,
      do the same things unto them,
      and
      give up threatening:
          knowing that
             He who is both their Master and yours is in heaven,
             and
             there is no respect of persons with Him.

6:10   Finally,
      be strong
            in the Lord,
            and
            in the strength of his might.

6:11   Put on the whole armor of God,
            that
            you may be able to stand against the wiles of the devil.

6:12   For
      our wrestling is
            not against flesh and blood,
            but
            against the principalities,
            against the powers,
            against the world-rulers of this darkness,
            against the spiritual hosts of wickedness in the heavenly places.

6:13   Therefore
      take up the whole armor of God,
            that
            you may be able to withstand in the evil day,
            and,
               having done all,
            to stand.

6:14   Stand therefore,
> having girded your loins with truth,
> and
> having put on the breastplate of righteousness,

6:15   and
> having shod your feet with the preparation of the gospel of peace;

6:16   in all taking up the shield of faith,
> with which you shall be able to quench all the fiery darts of the evil one.

6:17   and
take
> the helmet of salvation,
> and
> the sword of the Spirit,
>> which is the word of God:

6:18   with all prayer and supplication
praying at all seasons in the Spirit,
and
watching in all perseverance and supplication for all the saints,

6:19   and
on my behalf,
> that
> utterance may be given unto me in opening my mouth,
> to make known with boldness the mystery of the gospel,

6:20   for which
> I am an ambassador in chains;
that
in it I may speak
> boldly,
> as I ought to speak.

6:21   But
        that you also may know
            my affairs,
            how I do,
        Tychicus,
                the beloved brother
                and
                faithful minister in the Lord,
        shall make known to you all things:
6:22   whom
                I have sent unto you for this very purpose,
                        that
                        you may know our state,
                        and that
                        he may comfort your hearts.
6:23   Peace be to the brethren,
    and
    love with faith,
        from
                God the Father
                and
                the Lord Jesus Christ.
6:24   Grace be with all them that love our Lord Jesus Christ with a love incorruptible.

PHILIPPIANS - JOY IN THE JOURNEY

Chapter 1	Chapter 2	Chapter 3	Chapter 4
Paul's Thanksgiving in his Circumstances	Examples of True Servants	Warnings against False Servants	Final Exhortations and Rejoicing
• Thankfulness • Prayer • Exhortations	• Jesus • Timothy • Epaphroditus	• Paul (before his salvation) • Enemies of Christ	• Stand firm • Battling believers • Rejoice • Don't be anxious

Paul begins his message with thanksgiving. He is thankful to the Lord as he remembers the Philippian believers. He has been reminded of those Philippian believers by a gift that has come to him from them. Yet this is more than a mere thank you letter. Paul is thankful, not only for the fact of their gift, but that it means they are participating in the ministry of the gospel. It has been an ongoing participation. It started when they first came to Christ and it has continued through to the present.

There is a lesson here. It is that when someone really participates in the gospel through faith, the result will be that such a one will continue to participate in the gospel through their continuing actions.

Special Characteristics

• Paul writes this epistle from prison, yet it is an epistle filled with joy. The words "joy" and "rejoice" are found throughout the epistle.

• This epistle contains no quotations from the Old Testament. The believers in Philippi are mostly Greek and Roman and they are relatively unfamiliar with the Old Testament.

• Paul sends his thanks to this church for their gift of money to his ministry. At the same time, he shares how he has learned to be content both in poverty as well as in prosperity.

The Kenosis of Christ

Philippians 2:7 speaks of how Christ "emptied Himself." This description of the incarnation has been the source of debate with regard to our understanding of what was involved in the person of Jesus. Of what did He empty from Himself to take on flesh? To say that He emptied Himself of His deity would imply that He ceased to be divine. A better way of understanding it would be to say that Christ emptied Himself of His glorious prerogatives. This is explained in verse 8 that tells us "He humbled Himself."

1:1 Paul and Timothy,
   slaves of Christ Jesus,
  to
   all the saints in Christ Jesus that are at Philippi,
   with
     the overseers
     and
     deacons:
1:2 Grace to you
  and
  peace
   from
     God our Father
     and
     the Lord Jesus Christ.

1:3   I thank my God upon all my remembrance of you,

1:4   always
           in every supplication of mine
                on behalf of you all
        making my supplication with joy,

1:5   for your fellowship in furtherance of the gospel
           from the first day until now;

1:6   being confident of this very thing,
        that
        He
           who
           began a good work in you
        will perfect it
           until the day of Jesus Christ:

1:7   even as it is right for me to be thus minded on behalf of you all,
        because
        I have you in my heart,
           inasmuch as,
                both
                in my bonds
                and
                in the defense and confirmation of the gospel,
           you all are partakers with me of grace.

1:8   For
    God is my witness,
    how I long after you all
        in
        the tender mercies of Christ Jesus.

1:9   And
       this I pray,
          that
          your love may abound yet more and more
                in
                      knowledge
                      and
                      all discernment;

1:10   so that
       you may approve the things that are excellent;
          that
          you may be
                sincere
                and
                void of offence
          until the day of Christ;
1:11   being filled with the fruits of righteousness,
                    which are
                      through Jesus Christ,
                      unto the glory and praise of God.

1:12 Now
I would have you know,
 brethren,
that
the things which happened unto me
have fallen out rather unto the progress of the gospel;
1:13 so that
 my bonds became manifest in Christ
   throughout
   the whole praetorian guard,
   and
   to all the rest;
1:14 and that
 most of the brethren in the Lord,
  being confident through my bonds,
 are more abundantly bold to speak the word of God
  without fear.
1:15 Some indeed preach Christ even of envy and strife;
 and
 some also of good will:
1:16   the one do it of love,
    knowing that I am set for the defense of the gospel;
1:17   but
  the other proclaim Christ of faction,
   not sincerely,
   thinking to raise up affliction for me in my bonds.
1:18 What then?
Only that in every way,
 whether in pretense
 or
 in truth,
Christ is proclaimed;
and
therein I rejoice,
 yea,
 and will rejoice.

1:19   For
      I know that this shall turn out to my salvation,
         through
            your supplication
            and
            the supply of the Spirit of Jesus Christ,

1:20   according to
      my earnest expectation and hope,
  that
  in nothing shall I be put to shame,
  but that
      with all boldness,
      as always,
      so now also
  Christ shall be magnified in my body,
      whether
         by life,
         or
         by death.

1:21   For
  to me to live is Christ,
  and
  to die is gain.

1:22 But
    if to live in the flesh,
        – if this shall bring fruit from my work,
    then
    what I shall choose I know not.

1:23 But
    I am in a strait between the two,
        having the desire to depart and be with Christ;
            for
            it is very far better:

1:24   yet
    to abide in the flesh is more needful for your sake.

1:25 And
        having this confidence,
    I know that I shall abide,
        yes,
        and abide with you all,
            for
            your progress and joy in the faith;

1:26 that
    your glorying may abound
        in Christ Jesus
        in me
        through my presence
        with you again.

1:27   Only
    let your manner of life be worthy of the gospel of Christ:
        that,
            whether I come and see you
            or
            be absent,
        I may hear of your state,
        that you stand fast
            in one spirit,
            with one soul
            striving for the faith of the gospel;

1:28   and
    in nothing being frightened by the adversaries:
        which is
            for them an evident token of perdition,
            but
            of your salvation,
                and that
                from God;

1:29   because
            to you it has been granted in the behalf of Christ,
                not only to believe on him,
                but
                also to suffer in his behalf:

1:30   having the same conflict
        which
            you saw in me,
            and
            now hear to be in me.

2:1   If there is therefore any exhortation in Christ,
        if any consolation of love,
        if any fellowship of the Spirit,
        if any tender mercies and compassions,
2:2 fulfill my joy,
        that
        you be
            of the same mind,
            having the same love,
            being of one accord,
            of one mind;
2:3   doing nothing through faction or through empty-glory,
        but
            in lowliness of mind
       each counting other better than himself;
2:4   not looking each of you to his own things,
        but
            each of you also to the things of others.

2:5 Have this mind in you,
   which
   was also in Christ Jesus:

2:6   who,
     existing in the form of God,
     did not regard equality with God a thing to be grasped,

2:7   but
     emptied himself,
      taking the form of a servant,
      being made in the likeness of men;

2:8   and
      being found in fashion as a man,
     he humbled himself,
      becoming obedient
       even unto death,
       yes, the death of the cross.

2:9 Therefore also
  God
    highly exalted him,
    and
    gave unto him the name which is above every name;

2:10   that
     at the name of Jesus every knee should bow,
      of things in heaven
      and
      things on earth
      and
      things under the earth,

2:11   and that
     every tongue should confess that Jesus Christ is Lord,
      to the glory of God the Father.

2:12   So then,

         my beloved,

     even as you have always obeyed,

       not as in my presence only,

       but

       now much more in my absence,

  work out your own salvation

       with fear and trembling;

2:13   for

     it is God who works in you

       both

         to will

         and

         to work,

     for his good pleasure.

2:14   Do all things without murmurings and disputations:

2:15   that

     you may become

       blameless and innocent,

       children of God

         unblemished

         in the midst of a crooked and distorted generation,

           among whom

           you are manifested as lights in the world,

2:16   holding forth the word of life;

              that

              I may have reason to boast in the day of Christ,

                that

                I did not

                  run emptily

                  neither

                  labor emptily.

2:17   Yes,

  and if I am offered upon the sacrifice and service of your faith,

    I joy,

    and

    rejoice with you all:

2:18   and

  in the same manner you also have joy, and rejoice with me.

2:19   But
        I hope in the Lord Jesus to send Timothy shortly unto you,
            that
            I also may be of good comfort,
                when I know your state.

2:20   For
        I have no man like-minded,
                who
                will care truly for your state.

2:21   For
        they all seek
            their own,
            not the things of Jesus Christ.

2:22   But
        you know the proof of him,
            that,
            as a child serves a father,
            so he served with me in furtherance of the gospel.

2:23   Him therefore
        I hope to send immediately,
        so soon as I shall see how it will go with me:

2:24   but
        I trust in the Lord that I myself also shall come shortly.

2:25 But
I counted it necessary to send to you Epaphroditus,
> my brother
> and
> fellow-worker
> and
> fellow-soldier,
> and your messenger and minister to my need;

2:26 since he
> longed after you all,
> and
> was distressed,
>> because
>> you had heard that he was sick:

2:27
>>> for indeed
>>> he was sick near death:
>>> but
>>> God had mercy on him;
>>>> and not on him only,
>>>> but
>>>> on me also,
>>>>> that
>>>>> I might not have sorrow upon sorrow.

2:28 I have sent him therefore the more diligently,
> that,
> when you see him again,
> you may rejoice,
> and
> that I may be the less sorrowful.

2:29 Receive him therefore in the Lord with all joy;
and
hold such in honor:

2:30 > because
>> for the work of Christ
>>> he came near to death,
>>> hazarding his life to supply that which was lacking in your service
>>> toward me.

3:1 Finally, my brethren,
rejoice in the Lord.
   To write the same things to you,
      to me indeed is not irksome,
      but
      for you it is safe.

3:2 Beware of the dogs,
beware of the evil workers,
beware of the mutilation:

3:3   for
   we are the circumcision,
      who
      worship by the Spirit of God,
      and
      glory in Christ Jesus,
      and
      have no confidence in the flesh:

3:4   though
      I myself might have confidence even in the flesh:
      if any other man thinks to have confidence in the flesh,
      I yet more:

3:5   circumcised the eighth day,
         of the stock of Israel,
         of the tribe of Benjamin,
         a Hebrew of Hebrews;
         as touching the law, a Pharisee;

3:6   as touching zeal, persecuting the church;
         as touching the righteousness which is in the law,
           found blameless.

3:7   However
      what things were gain to me,
      these have I counted loss for Christ.

3:8   But indeed,
       also I count all things to be loss
       for the higher value of the knowledge of Christ Jesus my Lord:
                for whom
                I suffered the loss of all things,
       and
       do count them but refuse,
          that
             I may gain Christ,

3:9   and
             be found in him,
                not having a righteousness of my own,
                    even that which is of the law,
                but
                that which is through faith in Christ,
                    the righteousness which is
                        from God
                        by faith:

3:10   that
       I may know him,
          and
          the power of his resurrection,
          and
          the fellowship of his sufferings,
             becoming conformed unto his death;

3:11   if by any means I may attain unto the resurrection from the dead.

3:12   Not that
       I have already obtained,
       or
       am already made perfect:
    but I
     press on,
    if so be that I may lay hold on that
    for which also I was laid hold on by Christ Jesus.

3:13 Brethren,
  I count not myself yet to have laid hold:
  but
  one thing I do,
    forgetting the things which are behind,
    and
    stretching forward to the things which are before,

3:14 I press on toward the goal to the prize of the high calling of God
    in
    Christ Jesus.

3:15 Let us therefore,
  as many as are perfect,
  be thus minded:
    and
    if in anything you are otherwise minded,
    this also shall God reveal unto you:

3:16 only,
  whereunto we have attained,
  by that same rule let us walk.

3:17 Brethren,
   be imitators together of me,
   and
   mark them that so walk
     even as
     you have us for an example.

3:18 For many walk,
       of whom I told you often,
       and
       now tell you even weeping,
     that
     they are the enemies of the cross of Christ:

3:19   whose end is perdition,
       whose god is the belly,
       and
       whose glory is in their shame,
       who mind earthly things.

3:20 For
   our citizenship is in heaven;
     from where also we wait for a Savior,
       the Lord Jesus Christ:

3:21   who
       shall fashion anew the body of our humiliation,
        that
        it may be conformed to the body of his glory,
       according to
       the working whereby he is able
       even to subject all things unto himself.

4:1   Therefore,
        my brethren
        beloved
        and
        longed for,
        my joy and crown,
    so stand fast in the Lord, my beloved.

4:2   I exhort Euodia,
    and
    I exhort Syntyche,
    to be of the same mind in the Lord.

4:3   Yes,
    I beseech you also,
        true yoke-fellow,
    help these women,
        for
        they labored with me in the gospel,
        with Clement also,
        and
        the rest of my fellow-workers,
            whose
            names are in the book of life.

4:4   Rejoice in the Lord always:
    again I will say,
    Rejoice.

4:5   Let your gentleness be known unto all men.
    The Lord is at hand.

4:6   In nothing be anxious;
        but
        in everything
            by prayer
            and
            supplication
            with
            thanksgiving
        let your requests be made known unto God.

4:7   And
        the peace of God,
            which
            passes all understanding,
        shall guard your hearts and your thoughts in Christ Jesus.

4:8   Finally, brethren,
            whatsoever things are true,
            whatsoever things are honorable,
            whatsoever things are just,
            whatsoever things are pure,
            whatsoever things are lovely,
            whatsoever things are of good report;
            if there be any virtue,
            and
            if there be any praise,
        think on these things.

4:9   The things which you both
            learned
            and
            received
            and
            heard
            and
            saw in me,
        these things do:
            and
            the God of peace shall be with you.

4:10 But
 I rejoice in the Lord greatly,
  that
  now at length you have revived your thought for me;
  wherein you did indeed take thought,
  but
  you lacked opportunity.
4:11 Not that I speak in respect of want:
  for
  I have learned, in whatsoever state I am, therein to be content.
4:12 I know how to be abased,
 and
 I know also how to abound:
  in everything
  and
  in all things
 I have learned the secret
  both to be filled and to be hungry,
  both to abound and to be in want.
4:13 I can do all things in him who strengthens me.
4:14 However
 you did well that you had fellowship with my affliction.

4:15   And
you yourselves also know,
you Philippians,
that
in the beginning of the gospel,
      when I departed from Macedonia,
no church had fellowship with me in the matter of giving and receiving
but
you only;

4:16   for
      even in Thessalonica you sent once and again to my need.

4:17   Not that I seek for the gift;
but
I seek for the fruit that increases to your account.

4:18   But
I have all things, and abound:
I am filled, having received from Epaphroditus the things that came from you,
      an odor of a sweet smell,
      a sacrifice acceptable,
      well-pleasing to God.

4:19   And
my God shall supply your every need
      according to
      his riches in glory in Christ Jesus.

4:20   Now
unto our God and Father be the glory for ever and ever.
      Amen.

4:21   Salute every saint in Christ Jesus.
The brethren that are with me salute you.

4:22   All the saints salute you,
      especially
      they that are of Caesar's household.

4:23   The grace of the Lord Jesus Christ be with your spirit.

COLOSSIANS - CHRIST AS HEAD OF THE BODY

Chapter 1	Chapter 2	Chapter 3	Chapter 4
Doctrinal		**Practical**	
The Supremacy of Christ	The Fulness of Christ	The Image of Christ	Servants of Christ
What we are to believe about the person of Christ		How we are to live as a result of our union to Christ	

While Ephesians presents the church as the body of Christ, Colossians has its focus upon Jesus as the head of the body.

Warning against False Teaching

Paul speaks to problems in the church of Colossae that suggest doctrinal battles going on within the church. These battles reflected both the issues of Jewish legalism as well as Greek philosophy.

Galatian Heresy	Colossian Heresy
Faith is not enough for salvation	Christ is not enough for salvation

See to it that no one takes you captive through philosophy and empty deception, according to the tradition of men, according to the elementary principles of the world, rather than according to Christ (Colossians 2:8).

In contrast to this threatened captivity, Paul presents the gospel, pointing out how Christ has made men free, having paid their debt upon the cross and raising them to a new life. As a result, you are to let no one act as your judge in regard to food or drink or in respect to a festival or a new moon or a Sabbath day.

Practical Applications

Because you have been raised to newness of life, you are called to *set your mind on the things above, not on the things that are on earth* (3:2). This new way of thinking involves seeing yourself as having died to sin and putting on a new self that has its identity in the person of Christ.

Specific Instructions

Similar to the pattern found in the Epistle to the Ephesians, Paul gives specific instructions to a number of different groups within the church.
- Wives, be subject to your husbands, as is fitting in the Lord (3:18).
- Husbands, love your wives, and do not be embittered against them (3:19).
- Children, be obedient to your parents in all things (3:20).
- Fathers, do not exasperate your children, that they may not lose heart (3:21).
- Slaves, in all things obey those who are your masters on earth (3:22).
- Masters, grant to your slaves justice and fairness, knowing that you too have a Master in heaven (4:1).

1:1   Paul,
            an apostle of Christ Jesus
                    through
                    the will of God,
        and
        Timothy
            our brother,
1:2   To
            the saints
            and
            faithful brethren in Christ
        that are at Colossae:
        Grace to you
        and
        peace
            from God our Father.

1:3   We give thanks to God
        the Father of our Lord Jesus Christ,
praying always for you,

1:4   having heard
    of your faith in Christ Jesus,
    and
    of the love which you have toward all the saints,

1:5   because
    of the hope which is laid up for you in the heavens,
        by which
        you heard before in the word of the truth of the gospel,

1:6   which
            is come unto you;
            even as
            it is also in all the world
                bearing fruit
                and
                increasing,
            as it doth in you also,
                since the day
                    you heard
                    and
                    knew the grace of God in truth;

1:7   even as
                you learned of Epaphras
                    our beloved fellow-servant,
                    who is a faithful minister of Christ on our behalf,

1:8   who
                also declared unto us your love in the Spirit.

1:9 For this cause we also,
   since the day we heard it,
  do not cease
   to pray
   and
   make request for you,
  that
  you may be filled with the knowledge of his will
   in all spiritual wisdom and understanding,
1:10 to walk worthy of the Lord to all pleasing,
  bearing fruit in every good work,
  and
  increasing in the knowledge of God;
1:11 strengthened with all power,
   according to
   the might of his glory,
   unto all patience and longsuffering with joy;
1:12 giving thanks unto the Father,
   who
   made us qualified to be partakers of the inheritance of the saints in light;
1:13 who
   delivered us out of the power of darkness,
   and
   translated us into the kingdom of the Son of his love;

1:14   in whom we have
           our redemption,
           the forgiveness of our sins:

1:15   who is
           the image of the invisible God,
           the firstborn of all creation;

1:16   for
           in him were all things created,
              in the heavens and upon the earth,
              things visible and things invisible,
              whether thrones or dominions or principalities or powers;
           all things have been created
              through him,
              and
              unto him;

1:17   and
        he is before all things,
        and
        in him all things consist.

1:18   And
        he is the head of the body,
           the church:
         who is
        the beginning,
         the firstborn from the dead;
           that
           in all things he might have the preeminence.

1:19 For
    it was the good pleasure of the Father
      that in him should all the fulness dwell;

1:20   and
    through him to reconcile all things unto himself,
      having made peace through the blood of his cross;
    through him, I say,
    whether
      things upon the earth,
      or
      things in the heavens.

1:21   And you,
      being in time past
         alienated
         and
         enemies
            in your mind
            in your evil works,

1:22   yet now
      he has reconciled in the body of his flesh through death,
      to present you
         holy
         and
         without blemish
         and
         unreproveable before him:

1:23   if so be that you continue in the faith,
         grounded
         and
         steadfast,
         and
         not moved away from the hope of the gospel
            which you heard,
            which was preached in all creation under heaven;
         whereof
      I Paul was made a minister.

1:24   Now
        I rejoice in my sufferings for your sake,
        and
        fill up on my part that which is lacking of the afflictions of Christ
            in my flesh
            for his body's sake,
                which is the church;

1:25   whereof I was made a minister,
                according to
                the administration of God which was given me to you,
                    to fulfil the word of God,

1:26   even
                the mystery
                    which has been hid for ages and generations:
                    but now
                    has it been manifested to his saints,

1:27   to whom
                    God was pleased to make known
                    what is the riches of the glory of this mystery
                    among the Gentiles,
                        which is
                    Christ in you, the hope of glory:

1:28   whom
                        we proclaim,
                            admonishing every man
                            and
                            teaching every man in all wisdom,
                      that
                    we may present every man perfect in Christ;

1:29   whereunto
            I labor also,
            striving according to his working,
                which
                works in me mightily.

2:1   For
        I would have you know how greatly I strive
            for you,
            and
            for them at Laodicea,
            and
            for as many as have not seen my face in the flesh;

2:2   that
        their hearts may be comforted,
        they being knit together
            in love,
            and
            unto all riches of the full assurance of understanding,
        that
        they may know the mystery of God,
        even Christ,

2:3   in whom are hidden all the treasures of wisdom and knowledge.

2:4   This I say,
            that
            no one may delude you with persuasiveness of speech.

2:5   For
        though I am absent in the flesh,
        yet am I with you in the spirit,
            joying
            and
            beholding
                your order,
                and
                the steadfastness of your faith in Christ.

2:6   As therefore you received Christ Jesus the Lord,
so walk in him,
2:7   rooted
            and
            built up in him,
            and
            established in your faith,
even as you were taught,
            abounding in thanksgiving.
2:8   Take heed
        lest there shall be any one that make spoil of you
            through
                his philosophy
                and
                empty deceit,
            after the tradition of men,
            after the rudiments of the world,
            and
            not after Christ:
2:9   for
                in him dwells all the fulness of the Godhead bodily,
2:10   and
                in him you are made full,
                    who
                    is the head of all principality and power:
2:11   in whom
                you were also circumcised
                    with a circumcision not made with hands,
                    in the putting off of the body of the flesh,
                    in the circumcision of Christ;
2:12   having been buried with him in baptism,
                wherein you were also raised with him
                    through faith
                    in the working of God,
                      who
                      raised him from the dead.

2:13 And you,
> being dead
>> through
>>> your trespasses
>>> and
>>> the uncircumcision of your flesh,
> you, I say,
> he made alive together with him,
>> having forgiven us all our trespasses;

2:14
>> having blotted out the bond written in ordinances
>>> that was against us,
>>> which was contrary to us:
>> and
>> he has taken it out that way,
>>> nailing it to the cross;

2:15
>> having despoiled the principalities and the powers,
> he made a show of them openly,
>> triumphing over them in it.

2:16 Therefore,
> let no man judge you
>> in meat,
>> or in drink,
>> or in respect of
>>> a feast day
>>> or
>>> a new moon
>>> or
>>> a Sabbath day:

2:17
> which
> are a shadow of the things to come;
> but
> the body is Christ's.

2:18   Let no man rob you of your prize
        by a voluntary humility
        and
        worshiping of the angels,
        dwelling in the things which he has seen,
        vainly puffed up by his fleshly mind,

2:19   and
        not holding fast the Head,
           from whom
           all the body,
               being supplied and knit together
               through the joints and bands,
               increasing with the increase of God.

2:20   If you died with Christ from the rudiments of the world,
    why,
        as though living in the world,
    do you subject yourselves to ordinances,

2:21   Handle not,
                 nor taste,
                 nor touch

2:22   (all which things are to perish with the using),
    after the precepts and doctrines of men?

2:23   Which things have indeed a show of
        wisdom in will-worship,
        and
        humility,
        and
        severity to the body;
    but
    are not of any value against the indulgence of the flesh.

3:1   If then
      you were raised together with Christ,
      seek the things that are above,
            where Christ is,
            seated on the right hand of God.

3:2   Set your mind
                  on the things that are above,
                  not
                  on the things that are upon the earth.

3:3   For you died,
      and
      your life is hidden with Christ in God.

3:4   When Christ,
            who
            is our life,
      shall be manifested,
      then shall you also be manifested with him in glory.

3:5   Therefore
         put to death your members which are upon the earth:
              fornication,
              uncleanness,
              passion,
              evil desire,
              and
              covetousness,
                which is idolatry;

3:6   for which things' sake comes the wrath of God upon the sons of disobedience:

3:7   wherein you also once walked,
         when
         you lived in these things;

3:8   but now
         put them all away:
              anger,
              wrath,
              malice,
              railing,
              shameful speaking out of your mouth:

3:9   do not lie to one another;
         seeing that you
              have put off the old man with his doings,

3:10   and
              have put on the new man,
                that is being renewed unto knowledge
                after the image of him that created him:

3:11   where there cannot be
                Greek and Jew,
                circumcision and uncircumcision,
                barbarian, Scythian,
                bondman, freeman;
              but
              Christ is all,
              and
              in all.

3:12   Therefore,
put on,
      as God's elect,
      holy and beloved,
a heart of
         compassion,
         kindness,
         lowliness,
         meekness,
         longsuffering;

3:13   forbearing one another,
       and
       forgiving each other,
if any man have a complaint against any;
even as the Lord forgave you, so also do you:

3:14   and
above all these things put on love,
      which
      is the bond of perfectness.

3:15   And
let the peace of Christ rule in your hearts,
         to which also
         you were called in one body;
and
be thankful.

3:16   Let the word of Christ dwell in you richly;
      in all wisdom
         teaching
         and
         admonishing one another
            with
               psalms
               and
               hymns
               and
               spiritual songs,
      singing with grace in your hearts unto God.

3:17   And
>whatever you do,
>>in word
>>>or
>>in deed,
>do all in the name of the Lord Jesus,
>>giving thanks to God the Father through him.

3:18   Wives,
>be in subjection to your husbands,
>as is fitting in the Lord.

3:19   Husbands,
>love your wives,
>and
>do not be bitter against them.

3:20   Children,
>obey your parents in all things,
>for this is well-pleasing in the Lord.

3:21   Fathers,
>provoke not your children,
>that they be not discouraged.

3:22   Servants,
>obey in all things those who are your masters according to the flesh;
>>not with eye-service,
>>>as men-pleasers,
>>but
>>in singleness of heart,
>>>fearing the Lord:

3:23   whatsoever you do,
>work heartily,
>>as unto the Lord,
>>and
>>not unto men;

3:24   knowing that
>from the Lord you shall receive the reward of the inheritance:
>>you serve the Lord Christ.

3:25   For
>he who does wrong shall receive again for the wrong that he has done:
>and
>there is no respect of persons.

4:1   Masters,
        render unto your servants that which is just and equal;
        knowing that you also have a Master in heaven.

4:2   Devote yourselves to prayer,
        watching therein with thanksgiving;

4:3   praying for us also,
        that
        God may open unto us a door for the word,
        to speak the mystery of Christ,
            for which
            I am also in bonds;

4:4   that
        I may make it manifest,
        as I ought to speak.

4:5   Walk in wisdom toward them that are without,
        redeeming the time.

4:6   Let your speech be always
        with grace,
        seasoned with salt,
            that
            you may know how you ought to answer each one.

4:7   All my affairs shall Tychicus make known unto you,
          the beloved brother
          and
          faithful minister
          and
          fellow-servant in the Lord:

4:8   whom
     I have sent you for this very purpose,
          that you may know our state,
          and
          that he may comfort your hearts;

4:9   together with Onesimus,
          the faithful and beloved brother,
             who
             is one of you.
     They shall make known unto you all things that are done here.

4:10   Aristarchus
     my fellow-prisoner
salutes you,
and
Mark,
     the cousin of Barnabas
     (touching whom you received commandments;
     if he come unto you, receive him),

4:11   and
Jesus that is called Justus,
     who
     are of the circumcision:
these only are my fellow-workers unto the kingdom of God,
     men who have been a comfort to me.

4:12　　Epaphras,
　　　　　　who is one of you,
　　　　　　a servant of Christ Jesus,
　　　　salutes you,
　　　　　　always striving for you in his prayers,
　　　　　　　　that
　　　　　　　　you may stand perfect and fully assured in all the will of God.

4:13　　　　For
　　　　I bear him witness,
　　　　that he has much zeal
　　　　　　for you,
　　　　　　and
　　　　　　for them in Laodicea,
　　　　　　and
　　　　　　for them in Hierapolis.

4:14　　Luke,
　　　　　　the beloved physician,
　　　　and
　　　　Demas
　　　　salute you.

4:15　　Salute
　　　　　　the brethren that are in Laodicea,
　　　　　　and
　　　　　　Nymphas,
　　　　　　and
　　　　　　the church that is in their house.

4:16　　And
　　　　when this epistle has been read among you,
　　　　cause that it be read also in the church of the Laodiceans;
　　　　and
　　　　that you also read the epistle from Laodicea.

4:17　　And
　　　　say to Archippus,
　　　　　　Take heed to the ministry which you have received in the Lord,
　　　　　　that you fulfill it.

4:18　　The salutation of me Paul with mine own hand.
　　　　Remember my bonds.
　　　　Grace be with you.

PHILEMON - SLAVERY TO BROTHERHOOD

Slavery was a common practice in the ancient world. When the New Testament gives instructions to believers within their various levels of society, it also gives instructions to slaves. This means that there were slaves who came to Christ in faith, who became associated with the Christian church, and who remained within the confines of their slavery.

One such slave was Onesimus. He had belonged to Philemon, but had escaped from his slavery and had run away, eventually coming to Rome. It was there that he met Paul and became a Christian. As chance would have it, Paul also knew Philemon and had a special relationship with both master and slave. Paul is now sending Onesimus back to his former master with a letter. The letter is our epistle to Philemon.

1:1-3	1:4-7	1:8-22	1:23-25
Opening Greetings	Prayer of thanks for Philemon	Paul's Appeal on behalf of Onesimus	Concluding farewells

This epistle begins with typical greetings, though these are of a personal nature. They include names who we suspect are a part of the family of Philemon and they also include the church that meets in the house of Philemon.

Next Paul gives a prayer of thanks. He speaks of how he makes mention of Philemon in his prayers and how he is able to thank God for Philemon's love and his faith in Christ.

As Paul comes to the heart of the matter of his writing, he speaks of an appeal on behalf of a spiritual child he has sired while still a prisoner in Rome. This child is Onesimus. There is a slight play on words at the first mention of Onesimus. It is a play on the name of Onesimus. His name means "profit." Paul describes Onesimus as having been formerly useless to Philemon but now useful to Paul and to Philemon. Though a different Greek word is used here, there is a sense in which we could say that the profitable one had been formerly unprofitable to Philemon but was now profitable to both Philemon and to Paul.

Paul had found great use for Onesimus and his ministry, but Paul does not wish to keep Onesimus without Philemon's consent. Therefore he is sending Onesimus back to his former master.

Paul does not tell Philemon to free Onesimus. Instead, he suggests that Onesimus has come back to his former master, *no longer as a slave, but more than a slave, a beloved brother* (1:16). Yet this is not given as a command or by compulsion, but instead Paul appeals to Philemon's free will (1:14). He wishes Philemon to act in this matter as one who has the love of Christ and who demonstrates that love and faith toward all the saints.

1:1   Paul,
          a prisoner of Christ Jesus,
   and
   Timothy
          our brother,
   to Philemon
          our beloved
          and
          fellow-worker,

1:2   and
   to Apphia
          our sister,
   and
   to Archippus
          our fellow-soldier,
   and
   to the church in you house:

1:3   Grace to you
   and
   peace
          from
               God our Father
               and
               the Lord Jesus Christ.

1:4 I thank my God always,
> making mention of you in my prayers,

1:5 hearing
> of your love,
> and
> of the faith which you have
>> toward the Lord Jesus,
>> and
>> toward all the saints;

1:6 that
the fellowship of your faith may become effectual,
> in the knowledge of every good thing which is in you,
> unto Christ.

1:7 For
I had much joy and comfort in your love,
> because
> the hearts of the saints have been refreshed through you,
> brother.

1:8   Therefore,
        though I have all boldness in Christ to command you that which is befitting,
1:9   yet for love's sake I rather beseech,
                being such a one
                        as Paul the aged,
                        and
                        now a prisoner also of Christ Jesus:
1:10   I beseech you for my child,
                whom
                I have begotten in my bonds,
                Onesimus,
1:11   who
                        once was unprofitable to you,
                        but
                        now is profitable
                                to you
                                and
                                to me:
1:12   whom
                        I have sent back to you in his own person,
                                that is,
                                my very heart:
1:13   whom
                I would have kept with me,
                        that
                        in you behalf he might minister to me
                                in the bonds of the gospel:
1:14   but
                without your consent I would do nothing;
                        that
                        your goodness should not be as of necessity,
                                but
                                of free will.

1:15 For
    perhaps he was therefore parted from you for a season,
        that
        you should have him for ever;
1:16   no longer as a servant,
        but
        more than a servant,
        a brother beloved, specially to me,
        but
        how much more to you,
            both in the flesh
            and
            in the Lord.
1:17 If then you count me a partner,
receive him as myself.
1:18 But
if he
        has wronged you at all,
        or
        owes you anything,
put that to my account;
1:19 I Paul write it with mine own hand,
I will repay it:
        that I do not say to you
        that you also owe me your own self besides.
1:20 Yes, brother,
let me have joy of you in the Lord:
refresh my heart in Christ.
1:21   Having confidence in your obedience
        I write to you,
        knowing that you will do even beyond what I say.

1:22 But

prepare me also a lodging:

for

I hope that through your prayers I shall be granted to you.

1:23 Epaphras,

my fellow-prisoner in Christ Jesus,

salutes you;

1:24 and

so do

Mark,

Aristarchus,

Demas,

Luke,

my fellow-workers.

1:25 The grace of our Lord Jesus Christ be with your spirit.

Amen.

Manufactured by Amazon.ca
Bolton, ON